Lalita Ahmed
Indian Cookery

British Broadcasting Corporation

Published by the
British Broadcasting Corporation
35 Marylebone High Street
London W1M 4AA

ISBN 0 563 128747
First Published 1978
Reprinted 1979
© Lalita Ahmed 1978

Cover photographs by Terry Hardman

Printed in England by Belmont Press, Northampton

Contents

Bread

Roti, chapati or phulka	38
Paratha	39
Stuffed parathas	40
Puris	41

Daal or Dals   42

Sherbets

Shikangi or Nimboo Pani	43
Fresh Fruit Sherbet	43
Lassi	44
Salty Lassi	44
Spiced Grape Sherbet	44

Sweets

Kheer	45
Vermicelli Kheer	45
Ras Malai	46
Halwa Semolina	47
Carrot Halwa	47

Introduction

Indian food is now very familiar to most people in this country. Greater London alone has nearly 600 Indian restaurants. Curries have become part of many English families, everyday menus and they look as though they are here to stay.

Although I was born in India I have lived in Britain for the last 17 years. I have learnt to adapt many traditional dishes to suit my style of life here and also to allow for the availability of ingredients.

In my BBC1 *Pebble Mill* programmes I will be demonstrating how simple it is to make interesting, exciting and delicious Indian dishes. In this book I have included a variety of authentic Indian recipes which are fairly cheap to make and which will suit most English palates.

I have also included a special chapter on spices, their history, origin and their role in Indian cookery.

Indian desserts are normally rich and condensed and very sugary. They do not always appeal to the Westerner's taste. But for those adventurous cooks who would like to give them a try I have included a few very simple recipes.

'The way to a man's heart is through his stomach,' is a saying which I have heard often in this country. But I saw the proof of this a long time ago as a small girl in India. In a man's world, after all the wars had been fought, politics had been played, the future of mankind pondered on, the weary male returned home and nothing more was needed to make him feel welcome and wanted then a gracefully arranged, piping hot meal served by a cheerful wife. By the time he had finished his meal, the wife had won the battle, tipped the scale of politics and solved the future of mankind and thus ruled over all she surveyed.

Happy cooking.

Lalita Ahmed

Spices for Indian Cooking

Spices are aromatic, vegetable substances used mainly for seasoning food and increasing its flavour. The science of cooking with spices dates back to 300 BC and a chapter on the classification of spices and their combinations and value is included in the ancient book *Arthashastra*.

It has been proven by many eminent scientists of India, like Sir P. C. Ray, that the use of condiments in dishes is a necessity in tropical countries, particularly in non-vegetarian food. These spices act as an effective catalyst in digestion where the appetite is sluggish and digestion poor.

Spices are used in Indian cooking mainly to complement the flavour of the basic ingredients without destroying the nutritive value of the food.

It was to buy spices that early European traders first went to the East. Strangely enough, the orientals are now buying many of their spices from Europe because they are often far better in quality than those sold in their places of origin.

If there is an Indian food store near to you, you will probably find that the spices can be purchased there considerably cheaper than in supermarkets.

I have restricted my list of spices to those which I believe are essential if you wish to be versatile in the art of Indian cookery.

Kali Mirch (black pepper)

It is said that black pepper was the very first spice to be used by man and for many years remained an important article of trade between India and Europe. It grows in south-west India, Java and a number of other places. The pepper pod grows on a vine and black peppers are the berries which have been dried in the sun before they were ripe. The fleshy part of the berries shrinks to a black, hard, brittle seed.

The white pepper is the centre of the fully ripened berry. These are put in water and the outer shells removed, they are then dried and ground.

White pepper is milder than black pepper and has more aroma. White pepper is used where colour matters. Both are used internationally and are easily available in supermarkets and grocery stores.

Dalchini (cinnamon)

Another international spice which is chiefly grown in West India and Sri Lanka. It is said to contain powers to inspire love and was used in olden times as an aphrodisiac. It is widely used in cakes, puddings, pickles, chutneys, pulaus and meat, fish, and poultry curries. It is easily available in supermarkets and grocery stores.

Lavang or Long (cloves)

This spice is said to have been in use before the first Egyptian civilisation. Cloves are the unopened flowers of a tree which are dried in the sun. The main sources of cloves are East Africa, and the East Indies. They are used in curries, pulaus, for roasting pork, and in pickling. The whole cloves are easily available in Britain and ground cloves are also sold.

Elaychi (cardamom)

This spice is used extensively in oriental cookery, particularly in India, Pakistan and Ceylon. The main source of cardamom is the south-east tip of India known as the Malabar Coast.

Cardamom is the fruit of a reed-like plant found on the hills. The fruit is a pod which varies in size and length. The smaller variety is considered to be the best. The seeds inside the pod have a very pleasant, yet strong, aroma. Whole Cardamom seeds are included in some popular ranges of spices. The large Elaychi has a very dark and rough shell. It is used mainly in preparing powdered garam masala (see page 13). Meat, poultry and fish curries, sweets and pulaus and biryanis are flavoured by this spice. It is also eaten as a breath freshener, for making spiced tea and in paan, a kind of leaf eaten by Indians after a meal.

Tej Patta (bay leaf)

Bay leaves are used for flavouring only and not eaten. The bay tree is to be found growing all over the world, not only for its leaves but as an ornamental tree. Bay leaves are easily available.

Mirchi or Mirch (chilli)

There are many varieties of chilli but the smaller ones are usually considered to be the best. The green fruit is dried and changes to red in the process. When the chillies have been thoroughly dried they are powdered. Chilli powder is an essential ingredient in almost all Indian and Pakistani dishes.

Pickles are also made of either the red or green chillies. A pickle made from green chillies, lime and fresh ginger is very good for the digestion.

Simla Mirch or Badi Mirch (capsicum)

This is the large fleshy variety of the chilli family commonly known in Britain as red or green peppers. The ripe red pepper is dried and powdered to make paprika. This imparts a rich red colour to all food and has a mild flavour.

Zeera (cummin seeds)

The cummin is a herb of the caraway type and the seeds of the plant are used. There are two varieties of cummin. The white one is used, both whole and powered, in Indian cooking. Whole cummin seeds are used for garnishing dishes like dals. This is called Tadka. Cummin is used in liquors, pickles, sausages, cheeses, biscuits and in fried rice. In northern India, Zira Jal, that is an extract made with water and cummin, is used as an appetiser.

The other variety is a small black cummin called Shah Zeera. Shah meaning royal. It has a very distinct flavour and is used for making special rice and meat preparations like pulau, biryanis and meat dishes. It is stronger and sharper in smell than the white variety.

Dhania (coriander)

Coriander is sold in leaf, powdered or seed form. The green leaves of coriander, which compare to the English parsley, are used to garnish many Indian dishes. Powdered coriander is a must for most Indian dishes and is used in gravies, dals and vegetable dishes in particular. Coriander seeds are included in some popular ranges of herbs and spices available in supermarkets and are usually available in health stores.

Haldi (turmeric)

This comes from the root of a plant which grows in Bangladesh, India and the West Indies. The colour of the dried root varies from dark orange to a deep yellow but once powdered turmeric has a distinct yellow colour.

Turmeric is used in powder form in all curries, dals and vegetable dishes. It is also used as a substitute for saffron in colouring food. It is a very good preservative. Turmeric is now becoming available in supermarkets.

Adrak (ginger)

This also comes from the root of the plant and it is available, fresh, dried, and in powdered form. It is used for making biryanis, meat, fish and poultry curries, pickles, chutneys and preserves. A favourite of mine is ginger tea.

Lasun or Lehsun (garlic)

Garlic is grown in India and in southern parts of Europe. It can also be grown like an onion in the English garden. The English are rather frightened to use it due to its strong smell. But once you overcome this fear it is a wonderful spice. It is widely used in meat curries, vegetables, pickles, chutneys, sauces and breads.

Most greengrocers now stock garlic cloves and it can be bought in a powdered form.

Methi (fenugreek)

Fenugreek seeds come from the dried fruit of an annual grown in Indian and many European countries. The leaves of the plant are considered a great delicacy and it is a popular vegetable. The seeds are used to make sweet and sour pickles, preserves and many meat and vegetarian dishes.

You may have to go to an Indian food shop for this spice or a health food shop.

Sauf (aniseed)

These are the seeds of the anise plant which grows in India and Europe. Aniseed is used for making pickles, preserves, confectionery, desserts, cordials and liqueurs. Asians eat a few aniseed as a digestive agent after a meal. It also has a very pleasant smell and sweet taste.

Aniseed can be obtained from health food shops and Indian food shops.

Javitri and Jaiphal (mace and nutmeg)

Both mace and nutmeg come from different parts of the same tree. The seeds become nutmeg and the dried fleshy part of the fruit becomes mace.

Mace is used in many meat dishes and nutmeg is mainly used to flavour cakes and puddings.

Both are available in supermarkets.

Zafran or Keshar (saffron)

Known as the 'King of spices', saffron is very expensive to buy. The reason for this is because saffron is made from the dried styles of a flower of the crocus family. Each flower has only three styles. To make 1 lb of saffron it takes nearly 80,000 flowers. You do, however, only need to use a few strands of saffron to flavour puddings, pulaus and biryanis and to give them a beautiful yellow or dark orange colour.

Saffron is used in both Hindu and Muslim religious feast preparations and religious rites. It is used in herbal medicine and can usually be bought from chemist shops in Britain.

Rai or Sarson (mustard)

This is a very well-known spice which is grown throughout the world. Mustard is used for roasts, many vegetable and daal dishes, for pickles, chutneys, curries and for making sauces and dressings for salads.

Hing (asafoetida)

This is a kind of gum resin obtained from the root of some species of fesula. It has a very strong smell and is said to have medicinal properties. It is used to flavour many vegetable and daal preparations. You can buy this from any Asian food stores.

Till (sesame seeds)

These are very commonly used in breads, sweets and confectionery. In Indian cookery they are used for making gravies rich and thick. Sweets made from sesame seeds are called patti and laddos and are given to women who breast feed. The oil produced from the seed is used for making pickles, for frying and for making margarine. It also makes the Indian gingili oil.

Sesame seeds are usually obtainable from health food shops.

Kalongi (nigella seeds)

These little black seeds are used in bread, pickles, sauces and many curries. Generally they are used whole. They impart a very pleasant flavour to the dish. Nigella seeds are available from Asian food stores.

Curry Pat or Patta (curry leaves)

Curry leaves are very much like bay leaves and are used for flavouring only. They can be used green or dried. In southern India they are extensively used in meat, fish and vegetable dishes and they are used in many dry chutneys. Curry leaves are grown in India and Pakistan and are available in all Asian shops in Britain. Curry powder by the way is not the powdered leaves but a combination of spices.

The following spices are essential in making the dishes on the following pages.

Turmeric
Chilli powder
Paprika
Dhania powder (coriander)
Zeera powder (cummin)
Shah-Zeera whole (black cummin)
Garlic powder
Ground ginger
Garam masala powder – this is the powdered form of the recipe below.

Garam masala (whole)

This is the Indian equivalent of the English mixed spice and is made up in the following way:

3-4 cloves	2 large cardamom
6-8 whole black peppercorns	4-6 small cardamom
1 stick cinnamon	1-2 bay leaves

Garam masala can be brought in Asian shops ready mixed. Wherever garam masala is used in the following recipes you can use the bought mixture or make up your own.
These ingredients are sufficient for one curry only.

Ghee Ghee is clarified butter which can be bought in tins from Asian shops. It can be used for frying instead of oil.

A Typical Indian Meal

Sherbets
Meat curry
Vegetable curry
Dal
Raita or green salad
Rice
Bread
Sweet
Tea or coffee

Either the meat (gosht) or the vegetable curry should be with gravy, if the rice (chawal) is plain or fried.
If you are serving Biryani (fried rice and spiced meat cooked together) you need yoghurt (dahin), chutney or a dry curry, not too spicy.

Meat Dishes

Beef, Mutton or Lamb Korma (Meat Curry)

The taste of a good curry depends on the frying. The longer you fry the spices the better the taste but you must not burn them as this can make the curry bitter. The bones are added to increase the flavour of the gravy and should be removed before serving. If you like a lot of gravy you can increase the amount of water or if you like a dry curry then boil the gravy quickly at the end of cooking to reduce it.

$1\frac{1}{2}$ lb of any meat
A few meat bones
1 medium onion
1 5-oz carton natural
   yoghurt
Garam masala, whole
$\frac{1}{4}$ tsp black cummin
1 tsp chilli powder
1 tsp salt

$\frac{1}{2}$ tsp turmeric
1 tsp paprika
$1\frac{1}{2}$ tsp cummin powder
$1\frac{1}{2}$ tsp coriander powder
$\frac{1}{2}$ cup cooking oil or
$1\frac{1}{2}$ tbsp ghee
1 tsp ground ginger
1 tsp garlic powder
$2\frac{1}{2}$ cups water

Remove any fat, skin and gristle from the meat and cut and wash thoroughly. Slice the onion thinly and fry in the oil or ghee until golden brown. Add the whole garam masala and then the spices and meat and fry for a good 5-10 minutes until the meat is browned on all sides. Add the yoghurt and fry for another 5 minutes. Slowly the spices and yoghurt will separate from the oil and the oil will float on top. At this stage add the water and the bones.

Let the meat cook very slowly until it is tender (50 minutes to 1 hour). Take out the bones before serving.

Tomato Gosht (Meat and Tomato)

1½ lb any meat
1 medium onion
Garam masala, whole
½ tsp turmeric
1 15-oz can tomatoes
   or 2 tbsp tomato puree
   plus 2½ cups water
1½ tsp cummin powder

1 tsp chilli powder
1 tsp ground ginger
1 tsp garlic powder
1 green pepper
½ cup cooking oil
½ cup water
1 tsp salt

Slice the onion and fry in the oil until lightly browned. Add the whole garam masala and the spices. Gently fry for 1-2 minutes. Add the meat and fry for a further 5-6 minutes. Add tomatoes (if you use tomato puree add this with 2½ cups water) and salt and simmer for 3-4 minutes. Add the water and cook until the meat is tender (40-50 minutes). Add the sliced green pepper and simmer for a further few minutes until the pepper is soft.

Saag Gosht (Spinach and Meat)

1 lb any meat
1 5-oz carton natural
   yoghurt
1½ lb fresh spinach
Garam masala, whole
1½ tsp cummin powder
½ tsp turmeric
1½ tsp ground ginger

1 tsp garlic powder
½ cup oil
1 tsp salt
2 oz butter
1 large onion
1½ cups water
1 tsp coriander powder

Slice and fry the onion in the oil until golden brown. Add the whole garam masala and fry for 1 minute. Add the rest of the spices and the meat and yoghurt. Fry the mixture until the oil separates from the meat – about 10-15 minutes. Then add the water and cook until the meat is tender and the water has reduced (40-50 minutes). Wash the spinach leaves, remove the stems and chop the leaves thinly. Add the spinach and simmer the curry until the spinach is cooked and the oil again starts to separate. Add the butter and sprinkle some cold water on the top. Let the dish cook for 10 minutes. The butter gives this curry a lovely flavour.

Bhoona Gosht

Bhoona Gosht is normally served as a side dish and garnished with green, chopped coriander leaves and green chillies.

$1\frac{1}{2}$ lb any meat	1 tsp garlic powder
$\frac{1}{2}$ cup oil	$1\frac{1}{2}$ tsp ground ginger
1 tsp cummin powder	1 tsp salt
$\frac{1}{2}$ tsp turmeric	2 cups water
$\frac{1}{4}$ tsp powdered black pepper	1 green pepper
	2-4 tomatoes
$1\frac{1}{2}$ tsp powdered garam masala	2 large onions
	Juice 1 lemon

Cut the meat and onions into cubes, quarter the tomatoes and slice the green pepper. Heat half the oil and add the spices and salt. Fry gently for 1 minute. Add the meat and fry for 5 minutes. Add the water and cook until the meat is tender and dry (40-50 minutes). Put on one side.

Fry the onion in the remaining oil until soft but not brown. Add the cooked meat and sliced green pepper and tomatoes. Sprinkle on the lemon juice.

Meat Madras

1½ lb any meat
1½ tsp coriander powder
½ tsp turmeric
1 tsp cummin powder
6-10 curry leaves
1 small stick cinnamon
1 oz desiccated coconut
4 oz fresh or canned
  tomatoes
1 tsp garlic powder
1 tsp ground ginger

1 medium onion
¾ cup oil
2 cups water
1 tsp chilli powder
¼ tsp fenugreek seed
  (optional)
1 tsp cummin seed
  (optional)
½ tsp mustard seed
  (optional)
Salt

If you are using the optional fenugreek, cummin and mustard seeds they should be roasted for 1-2 minutes and ground with a pestle and mortar or in an electric grinder.

Slice the onion and fry in the oil until golden brown. Add the cinnamon stick, and curry leaves, then the spices and salt and fry for 1 minute. Add the meat. Fry for 3-4 minutes and then add the water. Let the meat simmer until tender (about 25-30 minutes). Add the coconut and tomatoes and the roasted seeds if used. Cook for another 25 minutes.

Pasinda

In this dish the meat is cut into thin slices or strips.

1½ lb any meat
1 5-oz carton natural
  yoghurt
2 oz ground almonds
1½ tsp ground ginger
1 tsp garlic powder
2 tsp cummin powder

Garam masala, whole
Juice ½ lemon
1 medium onion
½ cup oil
1½ tsp chilli powder
1 tsp black cummin

Cut the meat into narrow strips about 1½ inches long. Put the meat into a bowl and add yoghurt and all the ground spices, almonds, salt and lemon juice. Let it marinate for a good 4-6 hours. The longer you marinate the meat the better the flavour will be.

Chop the onion and fry in the oil. Add the whole garam masala and the marinated meat. Cover the pan with a lid and simmer until the meat is tender (40-50 minutes for lamb; 60-75 minutes for beef). Add a little water if needed.

Keema (Mince Curry)

1 lb mince	Garam masala, whole
1 5-oz carton natural yoghurt	1 tsp chilli powder
or 7-oz can tomatoes	½ cup oil
or 1 tbsp tomato puree	½ tsp turmeric
1 tsp ground ginger	½ tsp cummin powder
1 tsp garlic powder	1 tsp coriander powder
1 medium onion	1 cup frozen peas
1 tsp salt	or ½ cauliflower
	or ½ lb potatoes

If you are using cauliflower or potatoes cut them into small pieces. Slice the onions and fry in the oil until tender and just turning brown. Add the whole garam masala first and then the spices. Fry for 1 minute and add the mince, and potatoes if you are using them. Fry the mince for a further 2-3 minutes, then add the yoghurt or tomatoes or tomato puree. Cook for 15-20 minutes. If you are using peas add 5 minutes before end of cooking time. Add cauliflower 10 minutes before the end of cooking time.

The tomatoes, if you use them, will add a lot of moisture to the dish but if you use puree you will also need to add ½ cup water.

Spiced Chops

1½ lamb chops
1 5-oz carton natural
  yoghurt
2 tbsp lemon juice
1½ tsp black pepper,
  ground
1½ tsp cummin powder
2 tsp paprika

1 tsp garam masala
  powder
1 tsp chilli powder
1 level tsp turmeric
1 tsp salt
1½ tsp garlic powder
1½ tsp ground ginger
A little oil

Put the washed chops in a pan and sprinkle the spices one by one over them. Add the yoghurt. Add the 2 tbsp of lemon juice to the spices and yogurt and rub into the chops. Cover the pan and leave to marinate for 1 hour.

Line a grill pan with foil and arrange the chops on it. Grill them for 10-12 minutes turning occasionally and brushing with a little oil if necessary.

Kofta Curry (Mince balls)

In this recipe you can use 4 fresh tomatoes, 4-oz canned tomatoes or 1 level tbsp tomato puree instead of the yoghurt if you wish.

1 lb mince
½ tsp salt
2 tsp powdered garam
  masala
½ tsp chilli powder
1 tbsp breadcrumbs
½ tsp garlic powder
¼ tsp ground ginger

Gravy
1 medium onion

3 cups water
½ tsp ginger powder
½ tsp garlic powder
1 tsp cummin powder
1 tsp coriander
½ tsp turmeric
Garam masala, whole
½ cup oil
1 5-oz carton natural
  yoghurt

Mix together the mince, salt, garam masala powder, chilli, breadcrumbs, garlic and ground ginger. Leave on one side and make the gravy. Chop the onion finely or liquidise. Fry in the oil until golden brown. Add the whole garam masala. Fry for 1 minute. Add the remaining spices. Fry for a further minute and add yoghurt or tomatoes. Fry the mixture quickly until the oil starts to separate. Add 3 cups of water and salt and bring to boil. Then simmer the sauce gently.

Make small balls from the mince mixture, about the size of a golf ball, and slide them into the simmering sauce. The sauce will start to evaporate slowly and the mince balls will cook during this process. Normally when 1-1½ cups of gravy remains the curry is ready.

Other meat dishes

Tandoori	Tandoor is a Punjabi word for a special clay oven in which meat and bread is cooked.
Tikka	This is barbequed dried meat, seasoned with spices and cooked in a Tandoor oven or on charcoal.
Kebab	Minced meat with herbs, spices, onions, roasted on skewers.
Shami kebab	Meat mixed with spices, boiled, mashed and stuffed with onions and chillies. The mixture is made into small round balls and fried.
Boti kebab	These are the same as tikkas – boti means boneless meat pieces.
Skikampoor	These are the same as Shami kebabs.
Rogan Josh	Meat curry with nuts.
Mutton Dopiaza	A meat dish prepared with a lot of onion.

Poultry Dishes

Chicken Curry

1 chicken (3-3½ lb)	2 tsp coriander powder
1 medium onion	Garam masala, whole
½ cup oil	1 15-oz can tomatoes
1 tsp ground ginger	or 5-oz carton yoghurt
1 tsp garlic powder	1 tsp salt
1 tsp turmeric	1 tsp paprika
1½ tsp cummin powder	A little water

Cut and wash the chicken. Drain in a colander. You can put the giblets into the curry also if you wish but do not use the liver which has too strong a taste. Try to cut the chicken into clean jointed pieces. From one chicken you should get 2 thigh joints, 2 legs, 2 wing tips, 4 breast pieces and 4 pieces of carcase. The bones enrich the gravy. They can be removed once the curry is made. You can use the skin of the chicken if you wish or it is quite easy to remove.

Chop the onion into small even pieces and fry in the oil until golden brown. Add the whole garam masala and then the chicken pieces and all the spices. Stir for a few minutes. Add the yoghurt and fry until it is dry and the oil starts to separate from the mixture – approximately 10-15 minutes.

If tomatoes are used then fry the chicken in oil and spice mixture until the water from the chicken is dry and the oil separating. Then add the tomatoes and crush them so that there is a thick gravy.

For both mixtures continue to cook in a low flame until the chicken is tender. Add a little water if the mixture gets too dry before the chicken is ready.

Dry Chicken Bhoona Murg

1 chicken (3-3½ lb)
Juice of 1 lemon
1 small onion
1½ tsp cummin seed
1½ tsp aniseed (optional)
1½ tsp ground ginger
1 tsp garlic powder
1 5-oz carton natural
   yoghurt

½ nutmeg (optional)
3/4 strands mace
   (optional)
½ tsp black cummin
4 small cardamoms
1 tsp salt
1½ tsp black pepper
½ cup oil

Cut the chicken into small pieces, or cut the meat off the bone, and wash and drain thoroughly. Mix all the remaining ingredients (except onion and oil) together and rub into the chicken with the yoghurt. Marinate for 2-4 hours.

Pour the oil into a non-stick or heavy-based pan, fry the onion until golden brown. Add the chicken and marinate and fry well. Let all the moisture evaporate. Constant attention is needed to ensure that the mixture does not burn. Put the mixture in a baking dish and let it cook in the oven without a lid for 30-40 minutes at gas mark 3, 325°F.

Fish Dishes

Prawn Curry

1 lb prawns, peeled and
  cooked
1 large onion
1 green pepper
½ tsp turmeric
1 tsp cummin powder
1½ tsp powdered garam
  masala
½ tsp salt

½ tsp chilli powder
½ tsp coriander powder
1-2 green chillies
1 7-oz can tomatoes
  or 4 fresh tomatoes
1 tbsp ghee or ⅓ cup oil
1 tsp garlic powder
1 tsp ground ginger

Cut the green chillies into two pieces and halve the
fresh tomatoes if using. Chop the onion and fry in the
oil or ghee until tender. Add the spices and fry for 1
minute. Add the prawns and the tomatoes and fry
for a further 2 minutes. Add the green pepper cut into
quarters and cook for a further few minutes until the
pepper is cooked. Add the green chillies just before
taking the curry away from the stove.

Fish Curry

2 lb coley or mackerel
1 large onion
1 7-oz can tomatoes
1 tsp chilli powder
½ tsp turmeric
1 tsp cummin powder
2 tsp coriander powder

1 tsp salt
1 cup oil
2 tbsp ghee
A little water
1 tsp garlic powder
1 tsp ground ginger

Cut the fish into 2-inch pieces and fry them in the oil
for 1-2 minutes. Using the ghee fry the chopped

onion until tender. Add the spices and fry for a further minute. Add the tomatoes and salt and let the sauce cook for 3-4 minutes. Slide the fish pieces gently into the sauce so as not to break them up and simmer for 5-8 minutes. Add a little water if the gravy is too thick.

Fried Mackerel

2 large whole mackerel	1½ tsp turmeric
2 tsp chilli powder	1 lemon
1 tsp salt	Oil for deep frying

Clean the scales from the mackerel and clean inside. Wash thoroughly and cut into 4-5 slices about 2 inches long. Cover the slices with chilli powder, turmeric and salt and rub the spices well in. Leave to marinate for 10-15 minutes.

Put enough oil in a pan to just cover the fish pieces. I usually fry 3 or 4 pieces at a time in a small frying pan with a cover to stop the oil splashing. Fry the mackerel pieces on a medium flame for about 2-3 minutes on each side. Drain them on kitchen paper. Serve hot sprinkled with lemon juice.

Vegetable Dishes

Mixed Vegetable Curry

1 lb frozen mixed
  vegetables
1 small onion
  or 1 tsp cummin seed
1 tsp coriander powder
½ tsp turmeric
1 tsp chilli powder

½ tsp garam masala
  powder
Juice of ½ lemon
  or 1-2 tomatoes
2 tbsp oil
½ tsp salt

Chop the onion and fry gently in the oil until tender.
If you are using cummin seeds put them in the warm
oil and they will start to fry with a crackling noise.
Put the vegetables into the pan and sprinkle with the
spices one at a time to ensure an even distribution.
Stir the mixture well for 1-2 minutes. Add the chopped
tomatoes if used and cover. The vegetables should
cook for 7-10 minutes. If lemon juice is used pour
evenly over the vegetables before serving.

Aloo Ka Rasa (Potato Curry with Gravy)

This is a favourite dish of the Hindus of Uttar Pradesh
and is an inexpensive recipe to make. Aloo means
potato.

1-1½ lb potatoes
1 medium onion
  or 1 tsp cummin seeds
1 pinch asafoetida
  (optional)
1 tsp salt
½ tsp turmeric

1 tsp coriander powder
1 tsp chilli powder
Green coriander for
  garnishing
1 tbsp oil
1 7-oz can tomatoes

Fry the chopped onion or cummin seeds in the oil and add a pinch of asafoetida and the potatoes. Fry for 3 minutes. Add the spices and salt and fry for a further minute. Add tomatoes and $2\frac{1}{2}$ cups water. Cover and simmer for 5 minutes. The gravy will thicken slightly with the starch from the potatoes. When the gravy has reduced to about $1\frac{1}{2}$ cups remove from the heat and serve. Garnish with chopped green coriander leaves.

Aloo Gobi (Potato and Cauliflower)

1 small cauliflower	$\frac{1}{2}$ tsp salt
4 potatoes	$\frac{1}{2}$ tsp turmeric
1 medium onion	1 tsp coriander powder
2-3 tomatoes	1 tsp chilli powder
Juice of 1 lemon	1 tsp garam masala
2 tbsp oil	powder
1 pinch asafoetida (optional)	

Cut the cauliflower into small pieces, cut the potatoes into even-sized quarters, and chop the onion. Fry the onion until tender then add the potatoes and fry for 6 minutes. Add the cauliflower (gobi) and fry for 3 minutes. Add the salt and the spices and tomatoes. Cover and cook very slowly. The potatoes and cauliflower cook in their moisture and so it is not necessary to add water. When the potatoes are fully cooked (about 7-8 minutes) sprinkle with the powdered garam masala and lemon juice.

This curry can also be made with a combination of spinach and potato (Aloo palak), cabbage and potato, peas and potato, and green beans and potato.

Dahi Baigan (Aubergine and Yoghurt)

This is usually served as a side dish. Baigan is the Indian name for aubergine.

1 lb aubergines	1 tsp paprika
1 10-oz carton natural yoghurt	$\frac{1}{2}$ tsp salt
$\frac{1}{2}$ tsp black pepper	Oil for frying
1 tsp garam masala powder	$\frac{1}{4}$ tsp sugar

Beat the yoghurt and season it with salt and sugar. Put in a flat dish. Slice the aubergine into rounds and fry in the oil for 1-1$\frac{1}{2}$ minutes on each side. Drain the slices on kitchen paper and then slide them into the yoghurt. Sprinkle with the salt, garam masala powder, black pepper and paprika in that order.

Bhurta (Roast Aubergine Hotch Potch)

1 lb aubergine	$\frac{1}{2}$ tsp chilli powder
1 large onion	$\frac{1}{3}$ cup oil
1 oz fresh ginger	Green coriander leaves
2 cloves garlic	1 green chilli
1 7-oz can tomatoes or 4 fresh tomatoes	$\frac{1}{2}$ tsp salt

Roast the aubergine whole in the oven or grill. When soft remove the outer skin of the aubergine and mash the inside with a fork. Thinly slice the onion and fry in the oil until just tender. Add the chopped fresh ginger and chopped garlic. Add the aubergine to the onion and add salt, tomatoes and chilli powder. Let it cook for 8-10 minutes stirring continuously so that it does not stick to the pan. Garnish with coriander leaves and green chilli pieces. This is excellent served with Roti (Indian bread).

Raitas

Raitas are side dishes made with yoghurt as the base and using various vegetables. The process is very simple and raitas go beautifully with curries. They are also very good for the digestion.

Cucumber Raita

½ cucumber
1 small onion
¼ tsp salt
¼ tsp black pepper,
   freshly milled

¼ tsp sugar
1 8-oz carton natural
   yoghurt
Green coriander leaves
1 green chilli

Grate the cucumber and onion. Whip the yoghurt and add salt and sugar. Add the onion and cucumber and sprinkle with black pepper. Garnish with green coriander and green chillies.

Raita using a combination of tomato, green pepper, onion and celery can be made in exactly the same way as the above.

Celery and Walnut Raita

6 sticks celery
1 8-oz carton natural
   yoghurt
   or sour cream

¼ tsp sugar
¼ tsp salt
¼ tsp black pepper
2 oz chopped walnuts

Whip the yoghurt and add the salt, sugar, and freshly-milled black pepper. Finely chop the celery and add to the raita with the chopped walnuts.

Salads

Mixed Chopped Salad

1 medium green pepper
2 large carrots
2 medium beetroot
1 small onion
$\frac{1}{4}$ cucumber
4-6 leaves lettuce

3-4 tomatoes

Dressing
Juice 1 lemon
Salt and pepper
1 tsp sugar

Chop all the vegetables into small pieces. Mix the dressing and toss all the vegetables in this, mixing firmly by hand.

Pyaz Ke Lachhe (Onion slices)

1 large onion
2 tomatoes
Juice 1 lemon

Salt and pepper
    or 1 tsp chilli powder

Thinly slice the onions and tomatoes. Mix them together with the lemon juice and seasonings, squashing them together gently. This can be eaten with all kinds of kebab and roasts, barbequed meats and with curries.

Rice Dishes

Rice is the staple food of many Asian countries but while it is rich in carbohydrate it is deficient in proteins and many essential minerals and vitamins. That is why pulaus, khichris and biryanis are more nourishing than plain boiled rice.

There are many kinds of rice grown in various parts of the world but the best rice is basmati which is grown only in India and Pakistan. This is lower in starch than other varieties and is long grained. The older the rice is the better it is. Next best is American long-grained rice. These rice varieties should be used for making boiled rice, rice salads, pulaus and for stuffing green peppers. Patna rice comes third in quality and is often used by restaurants because it is cheaper than the first two varieties.

$1\frac{1}{2}$ heaped cups of rice is the usual amount needed for two adults. 1 cup of rice will feed three children. Basmati rice when cooked soaks up $1\frac{3}{4}$ times its weight of water whereas Patna rice uses an equal amount of water to rice.

Basmati rice

This rice can only be bought from Asian stores. It is a little more expensive than other varieties but it is worth it. It has a lovely smell when cooked and is light and fluffy. All biryanis and pulaus are best made from this rice.

1 lb Basmati rice should be cleaned to remove any stones and washed thoroughly three or four times, rubbing gently between the palms. Good Basmati when rubbed and washed will appear bright and nearly transparent yellow in colour. There are two methods of cooking Basmati rice. For the first

method measure the rice in a cup before washing and then add $1\frac{3}{4}$ times that number of cups of water. This includes a little extra water to allow for evaporation.

I always put 4-5 drops of lemon juice and $\frac{1}{4}$ tsp of salt into the water. This helps to make the rice grains white and separate. Turn down the flame to very low and simmer until the rice is cooked (2-4 minutes). To test pick up a grain of rice and press. It should be quite soft with no hard bit in the core.

For the second method to 1 lb rice and 4-5 cups water add $\frac{1}{4}$ tsp salt and a little lemon juice and boil. When the rice is cooked strain out the water, cover the pan and leave the rice over a low flame for 1 minute. Serve in open dish with a lump of butter.

Use the second method for cooking Patna rice and other varieties of rice.

Fried Rice or Pulau

3 cups basmati rice	Garam masala, whole
2 tbsp butter, ghee or oil	$5\frac{1}{2}$ cups water
1 small onion	1 tsp salt

Clean and wash the rice. Slice the onion thinly and fry in the oil or butter until golden brown. Add the garam masala and rice and fry for 1 minute. Add salt and water. Let the water come to the boil and then lower the flame. Cook the rice until tender (about 10-15 minutes). Turn over the rice a couple of times with a spoon and then cover and leave to cook for another minute to allow all the moisture to evaporate.

Pulau rice can be coloured by adding 5-6 strands of saffron dissolved in 1 tablespoon warm water or milk to the cooked rice. Let the rice simmer for a further minute to let all the moisture evaporate. Instead of saffron you could use 1 teaspoon turmeric or edible yellow colouring.

You can also add the following ingredients to pulaus if you wish:

Green peas: add 1 lb frozen peas after the water has been added.

Potatoes: fry 1 lb potatoes in the oil for 3 minutes before adding the garam masala to the onion.

Spiced pulau: add ½ tsp garlic, 1 tsp ground ginger, ½ tsp chilli powder and 1 tsp turmeric to fried onion.

Mixed vegetable: add 1 lb frozen mixed vegetables after water.

Meat Pulau

3 cups rice (1½ lb)	Garam masala, whole
2 lb shoulder of lamb	1 tsp salt
1 medium onion	7½ cups water
1½ tsp ground ginger	2 tbsp butter, ghee
1 tsp garlic powder	or oil
1 tsp cummin powder	

Cut the bone from the shoulder of lamb and cut the meat into 1-inch pieces. Wash the meat and put in a pan with the salt, half the garlic and ground ginger and garam masala and water. Simmer the meat for 30-50 minutes on a medium flame. Let the water reduce to nearly 5½ cups and test if the meat is tender. The meat should feel really soft when pressed.

Now take another pan and heat the butter or oil. Fry the thinly sliced onion until golden brown. Add the remaining spices and washed rice. Fry for 1 minute and add the cooked meat and 5 cups of the stock.

The Pulau should be stirred once or twice only to ensure that the meat, stock and rice is evenly mixed but making sure the rice does not break.

Continue to cook on a very low flame for 10-15 minutes.

Shahi Pulau

3 cups basmati rice	$\frac{1}{2}$ tsp garlic powder
$5\frac{1}{2}$ cups water	$\frac{1}{2}$ tsp ground ginger
1 medium onion	Garam masala, whole
1 large potato	1 tsp salt
$\frac{1}{2}$ cup peas	$\frac{1}{2}$ cup butter, ghee or oil
$\frac{1}{4}$ cup carrots	1 small can pineapple
2 oz raisins	chunks
4 oz cashew nuts or almonds	

Clean and wash the rice and soak in $5\frac{1}{2}$ cups water. Fry the thinly sliced onion in the oil or butter until golden brown. Add the whole garam masala, ginger, garlic and vegetables. Gently fry for 5-7 minutes. Add the nuts and raisins and salt. Drain the rice, saving the water and add to the pan and fry carefully for 1 minute taking care not to break the soaked rice. Add the pineapple pieces and water. Let the pulau cook on a low flame until the water is absorbed and the rice is soft.

Biryani

Biryani can be made in two different ways. One method is to cook the meat first and then add it to the cooked rice. The second method is called 'kachie gosht ki biryani' where the uncooked meat and rice are cooked together. Biryani is a very exotic dish which does not normally require many complimentary dishes. It is different to pulau in that spiced meat is used rather than seasoned meat and they both have a very different flavour.

When serving a biryani it is not necessary to accompany it with anything other than a raita, a salad or chutney. Although for a larger party you could serve a curry with a biryani.

In India biryani is a festive dish and is served at marriages and for large parties. Muslims especially make it during their two main festivals called Eids.

I have given a recipe using beef but you can use any other kind of meat, chicken, turkey, prawns, pheasant and even mince.

The ratio of meat and rice in biryanis varies depending on the purse, requirement and taste of individuals. There is a general rule that the meat or fish should be $1\frac{1}{2}$ times the weight of the rice.

Biryani (method 1)

$1\frac{1}{2}$ lb basmati rice
$2\frac{1}{4}$ lb beef
1 medium onion
2 garam masala, whole
2 5-oz cartons natural yoghurt
3 tsp salt
1 tsp turmeric
2 tsp cummin powder
$\frac{1}{2}$ bunch green coriander
$1\frac{1}{2}$ tsp garam masala powder

1 tsp chilli powder
Juice of 1 lemon
1 tsp black cummin
$1\frac{1}{2}$ tsp ground ginger
$1\frac{1}{2}$ tsp garlic powder
2 tbsp ghee, butter or $\frac{3}{4}$ cup oil
2 green chillies
$\frac{1}{4}$ cup milk
Saffron or edible yellow colouring

Measure the rice into cups and soak it in $2\frac{1}{2}$ times that amount of water.

Melt the ghee, oil or butter in a pan and fry the sliced onion until golden brown. Add 1 whole garam masala. Fry for 1 minute to season the oil and add the garlic and ginger. Add the turmeric, cummin, chilli powder and salt. Fry for 1 minute and add the meat. Stir 3-4 times and add yoghurt. Cover the pan and let the meat cook for 40 minutes to 1 hour. You may have to add $\frac{1}{2}$ cup water to cook the meat if the yoghurt has failed to do so. Remove the meat from the pan and put on one side.

Wash and clean the green coriander, chop the leaves and softer stalks. The thicker stalks should be discarded.

Take another pan large enough to accommodate the meat and rice together. Put in the soaked rice and half the salt, the second garam masala and black cummin. As the rice is presoaked it will cook very quickly in only 4-5 minutes. When the rice is almost cooked, ie, when it is pressed there is still a hard core and feels firm, quickly drain off the water and put half of the rice in a separate dish.

Spread the remaining rice over the base of the pan and add the meat. Make the layer of meat flat and do not add any of the gravy or oil. Cover the meat with half the powdered garam masala, green coriander and green chilli.

Add the remaining rice on top of this layer and sprinkle the remaining coriander leaves, chillies, powdered garam masala and lemon juice on top. If you are using saffron dissolve it in the milk and sprinkle on top. Or add a little yellow colouring.

Make 5-6 holes in the mixture with the handle of a ladle so that the steam can rise easily. Pour over the gravy and oil which the meat was cooked in and cover the pan.

Put the pan on a medium flame for $\frac{1}{2}$ minute to form steam then lower the flame as low as possible. Let the biryani cook slowly for 5-6 minutes. It is also possible to do this in a casserole dish in the oven.

Before serving mix the biryani from one side, mixing the top layer of rice evenly with the meat.

Biryani (method 2)

Use the same ingredients as method 1.

Mix the meat, yoghurt and all the spices and salt and let it marinate until required.

Wash the rice and put to soak in 3 times more water. Add 1½ tsp salt and whole garam masala and cook until the water boils. Partly cook the rice for approximately 2 minutes. It is difficult to give an exact time as varieties of rice vary. But the rice should remain hard but will have absorbed some of the water. Strain the rice and keep on one side.

Fry the onions until golden brown and remove the remaining oil from the pan.

Strain off the water keeping it on one side. Add the fried onions to the marinating meat. Take a large dish. Heat the oven to gas mark 4, 350°F. Put a little oil in the bottom of the pan and add the mixture of meat evenly so that it covers the base. Gently spread all the cooked rice over it covering all the meat. Then sprinkle the lemon juice all over and sprinkle with saffron or yellow colouring. Add a few green chillies, chopped green coriander leaves and the oil in which the onion was fried.

Take the long end of the ladle and make 6-8 holes in the rice for steam to rise. Cover with a firm lid, so that the steam does not escape. I normally cover the top with a clean tea towel and then the pan lid.

Let the biryani cook in the oven for 40 minutes to an hour. Do not stir during this process. Test the rice after 40 minutes, it is done when it has no hard core left.

Take a big flat server and gently lift the meat from the bottom of the pan and mix it with the rice on top, mixing from one side of the dish only. The art of serving biryani is to ensure that each individual gets whichever part of the biryani he most likes. There will be white, yellow and deep red rice depending on its position in the pan and pieces of spiced meat dotted throughout.

Many people add a few drops of rose water or kewra water to the rice just before serving.

Bread

There are three main forms of Indian bread – Roti (also called chapati or phulks); paratha and puri.

Roti, chapati or phulka

India is a vast country and the people there speak many different languages and dialects. This is why you get bread called roti in the north and chapati in the south. The southerners tend to make their chapati a little thinner than the northern roti. Roti is best made with wholewheat flour. It is a plain bread eaten daily in India with meat and vegetable curries. Butter or ghee can be spread on one side if you wish.

1 lb wholewheat flour	1-1½ cups water or
½ tsp salt	milk and water mixed

Sift salt and flour together and make dough by gradually adding small quantities of water. Knead the mixture well until all the flour is absorbed and dough is soft but not sticky. If it does become sticky rub your hands with some ghee or butter and sprinkle on the little extra flour while kneading the dough.

Cover the dough with a wet cloth or keep it in a container until you are ready to cook the bread.

Make the dough into approximately 1-oz balls. 1 lb dough will make about 16 rotis. Roll out each ball into fairly thin rounds (although this is a matter of personal preference). Place a flat frying pan onto a medium flame and when hot put in the roti one at a time cooking for about ½ minute on each side.

Both sides will have little dark specks on them. That is the time to put the roti onto a direct flame. To do this keep two gas rings alight side by side. When the roti is put from the pan onto the open flame it bloats. Turn upside down and take away from the flame. Apply a little butter or ghee and keep in a container lined with a clean cloth. Stack the rotis on top of each other, covering with the cloth each time to keep them warm and soft.

If you have an electric stove the rotis can be bloated in the frying pan. After frying, press the roti gently with a cloth and the steam from the roti bloats it. This method, however, takes a little practice.

Sometimes a little oil or butter is applied to the rolled dough. This makes a soft roti which keeps supple even after becoming cold.

Paratha

1 lb wholewheat flour	1-1$\frac{1}{2}$ cups water or
$\frac{1}{2}$ tsp salt	milk and water mixed

Sift salt and flour together and make dough by gradually adding small quantities of water. Knead the mixture well until all the flour is absorbed and dough is soft but not sticky. If it does become sticky rub your hands with some ghee or butter and sprinkle on the little extra flour while kneading the dough.

Cover the dough with a wet cloth or keep it in a container until you are ready to cook the bread.

Roll the dough into small rounds. This mixture should make about 16. Smear ghee liberally all over then fold it across and once more making a triangle.

Dip the triangle in flour and roll out into a large thin triangle. Put the frying pan over a medium flame and put in the paratha. Turn over when little brown specks appear, add a little ghee to the second side and fry until brown and crisp. Make the rest like this and keep one on top of another.

The paratha can be made round. You roll the dough into a large round. Smear ghee all over. Start rolling over one end and go on folding into a long roll. Now fold this roll into a compact circle. Flatten with hand and put some flour around it, by dipping it in the flour and roll out into a thin round shape. Fry as above.

Stuffed Parathas

Sometimes parathas are stuffed with vegetables and meat. They make excellent snacks. Here are some very tasty stuffings for parathas. They are all made in the following way:

Take a dough ball into your left palm and make a hollow in it. Place a lump of filling large enough to fit in the hollow and press it down. Pull the sides up and close the opening at the top. Roll the ball gently between your palms to make it nicely round. Then dip it in flour and roll it out gently into a round. Do not allow the stuffing to break out of the dough case. Then fry the paratha.

1. Mash 1 lb potatoes and add $\frac{1}{4}$ tsp salt, $\frac{1}{4}$ tsp black pepper, $\frac{1}{4}$ tsp chilli powder, coriander leaves chopped, 1 tsp whole cummin seeds, and a few drops of lemon juice or vinegar.
2. 8 oz grated cheddar cheese.
3. 8 oz frozen green peas, mashed coarsely and fried in a teaspoon of oil with $\frac{1}{4}$ tsp salt, $\frac{1}{4}$ tsp chilli, 1 tsp cummin seed, a little fresh ginger (chopped finely), seasoned with lemon juice and green coriander leaves.
4. 4 oz cooked mince (I usually use any mince left-over from other dishes).
5. 4 finely chopped hard-boiled eggs, seasoned with 2-3 lightly fried chopped onions, 1 green chilli, a little ginger and fresh coriander and $\frac{1}{2}$ tsp salt.

Puris

These are deep-fried small rotis.

1 lb wholewheat flour	1-1½ cups water or
½ tsp salt	milk and water mixed

Sift salt and flour together and make dough by gradually adding small quantities of water. Knead the mixture well until all the flour is absorbed and dough is soft but not sticky. If it does become sticky rub your hands with some ghee or butter and sprinkle on the little extra flour while kneading the dough.

Cover the dough with a wet clean cloth or keep it in a covered container until you are ready to cook the bread. Divide the dough into small balls. 1 lb flour makes 32 balls. Dredge the balls with dry flour and roll out into rounds approximately 3-4″ in diameter.

Heat enough ghee or oil in a pan to deep-fry the puris. Lower the heat a little and slide the puris into the pan one by one. Let them fry until they bloat. Turn over and fry till the thick side is golden. Pressing down lightly with a flat spoon with a circular movement helps to bloat the puris. Drain off any excess ghee and keep stacked on a plate. Puris are best eaten freshly fried.

Other breads

Kulcha	Deep-fried yeasted bread
Nan	Bread made with fermented refined flour and baked in clay ovens
Papadum	Crisp cracked rounds usually made of flour or potatoes or pulses and deep-fried or roasted

Daal or Dals

Dals are an essential part of an Indian meal. They are the main supply of protein. When essential foods like cheese, eggs, milk, fresh vegetables and fruits are beyond the reach of someone or in short supply sprouted pulses are a good substitute. Pulses or dals supply iron, phosphorus, and vitamin B and protein. As lentils are easily available here, I am giving you a simple recipe for lentil daal.

Lentil Daal

2 cups water	$\frac{1}{4}$ tsp turmeric powder
1 cup lentils	$\frac{1}{2}$ green chilli
2-3 fresh or tinned tomatoes	$\frac{1}{2}$ tsp coriander powder
	1 small onion
$\frac{1}{4}$ tsp salt	$\frac{1}{2}$ tbsp butter

Clean the lentils of stones and wash thoroughly. Put in pan with water and bring to the boil. Add sliced chilli, salt, sliced tomatoes, turmeric and coriander. Simmer until the lentil has dissolved in the water to make a thick mixture. Use a masher or a beater if necessary to make the daal smooth. Fry the finely chopped onions in butter until brown and pour over the daal. Serve with rice or bread.

Sherbets

Sherbets are very simple to make and when mixed with alcohol can make a very interesting start to a meal. They can also be made without the alcohol.

Shikangi or Nimboo Pani (Lemon Sherbet)

8 glasses water
32 tsp sugar
Juice of 2 lemons
Rind of $\frac{1}{2}$ lemon
Mint leaves (fresh)

$\frac{1}{2}$ cup vodka or gin
  (optional)
Crushed ice
$\frac{1}{2}$ tsp salt

Take a bowl or a pan and dissolve the sugar and salt in 8 glasses of cold water. Add lemon juice, lemon rind and a few mint leaves. Add the alcohol if desired. Serve with crushed ice. Makes a very refreshing long cool drink.

Fresh Fruit Sherbet

1 banana
1 orange
$\frac{1}{2}$ lb strawberries
1 apple
Few red or white grapes
Mint leaves (fresh)
Seeds of 4 small
  cardamom

$\frac{1}{2}$ bottle lemonade
Juice of 2 lemons or
  orange squash
1 litre water
2 cups sugar

Slice the banana into thin rings, peel and slice orange into rounds, halve the strawberries, core and slice the apple into rings and stone and halve the grapes. Put the fruit into a bowl and add lemonade and lemon juice (or squash), cardamom seeds, ice and a few mint leaves.

In a separate bowl dissolve the sugar and water. Pour over the fruit and serve with crushed ice.

Lassi

18 tsp sugar	Mint leaves
6 glasses water	12 oz natural yoghurt
$\frac{1}{4}$ tsp salt	

Take a mixing bowl, pour in the yoghurt and whip with a mixer. Add sugar, salt and water. Keep on mixing until the mixture is light and frothy. Serve on a bed of ice. Float a few mint leaves on top. Lassi means buttermilk.

Salty Lassi

1 tsp salt	12 oz natural yoghurt
$\frac{1}{4}$ tsp black pepper	6 glasses water

Whip the yoghurt and water together until frothy. Add salt and black pepper. Serve with ice.

Spiced Grape Sherbet

2 cups grapes	$\frac{1}{4}$ tsp black pepper
4 cups water	$\frac{1}{4}$ tsp salt
2 tbsp sugar	ice cubes

Into a liquidiser, put the washed and stoned grapes, salt and sugar and liquidise thoroughly. Pour the mixture into a pan and add the water. Stir thoroughly and then strain the sherbet through a sieve.

Serve the sherbet with ice in tall glasses with freshly ground black pepper on top.

Sweets

Kheer (Rice Pudding)

1 can rice pudding	Seeds of 6 small
1 pt fresh milk	cardamom
2 oz sugar	1 bay leaf
1 oz blanched almonds	2 oz sultanas
	$\frac{1}{2}$ oz pistachios

Put the bay leaf and milk in a pan and boil until the milk is reduced to half a pint. Add sugar and sultanas and let it cool. Powder the cardamom seeds with a rolling pin and stir in.

Add the cold milk mixture to the rice pudding and put in a serving dish. Cover the surface with sliced pistachios and sliced almonds. Refrigerate for a short while and serve cold.

Vermicelli Kheer

2 oz vermicelli	Seeds of 6 small
2 pts milk	cardamom
2 tsp butter or ghee	1 oz pistachios
1 bay leaf	2 oz sultanas
1 oz almonds	$\frac{1}{2}$ cup sugar
	4-6 dates

Reduce the milk to $1\frac{1}{2}$ pints by boiling rapidly. Put the butter or ghee in a pan. Melt it gently and add the bay leaf. Add the broken vermicelli and fry for 1 minute. Add the milk, sugar and sultanas and cook gently for 10 minutes. Add the stoned and sliced dates. Pour the pudding in a serving dish. Decorate with almonds and pistachios and sprinkle with the crushed cardamom seeds.

Ras Malai

5 pts milk
1½ level tsp plain flour
Juice of 1 lemon
1½ lb sugar
6 sugar cubes
1 oz almonds

1 oz pistachios
8 small cardamom
  seeds
4 drops rose essence or
  rose water

Put 4 pts milk in pan and bring to boil. Pour in the lemon juice. Turn off the heat and let the milk separate into cheese. Stand for 5-10 minutes. Using a sieving cloth or muslin strain the separated milk mixture. Tie up the cheese in the cloth and leave overnight so that every single drop of water has gone.

With your palm rub the cheese so that every globule is crushed. Slowly sprinkle with flour and keep on rubbing the cheese for at least 10 minutes. Cover mixture with a clean damp cloth so that it does not become dry.

Put the sugar and ¾ pints water into pan and boil. Let the sugar syrup simmer gently.

Now take a small round of cheese: make it into a round ball about the size of a 2p coin. Make a depression in the middle and put one quarter of a sugar cube in it. Cover the cube with cheese and lightly press it to flatten it. Make about 6 of these and slide them into the gently boiling syrup. Let these cook for 15 minutes. Add remaining mixture 6 rounds at a time. Keep on adding spoonfuls of water to the edge of the pan to replace the evaporated water from the syrup. Sometimes the syrup becomes thick and gives the Ras Malai a yellow colour.

When cooked these cheese sweets will be almost twice their size.

Boil the remaining pint of milk and reduce to ¾ pint. Arrange the cheese sweets in a shallow serving dish. Add rose water and cardamom crushed seed to the thickened milk and pour over the Ras Malai. Sprinkle

with chopped nuts and refrigerate. This sweet can be
kept in the fridge for 3-4 days, or can be frozen.

Halwa Semolina

6 oz coarse semolina   1 oz raisins or sultanas
6 oz butter or ghee   6 cardamom seeds
14 oz water   3 oz sugar
1 oz almonds

Melt the butter gently in a pan. Add semolina and fry
until it turns slowly reddish brown. This takes about
10-12 minutes. Turn the semolina constantly to roast
every particle. When the semolina begins to change
colour add sugar and raisins and stir in water. Lower
heat and cover pan with lid. Stir the halwa occasionally.
When the semolina has soaked up the water and the
halwa (pudding) is brown add the crushed cardamom
seeds. Put in a serving dish and decorate with chopped
almonds. Serve hot or cold.

Carrot Halwa

3 lb carrots $1\frac{1}{2}$ lb sugar
2 oz sultanas $\frac{1}{2}$ lb butter or ghee
2 oz almonds   2 pints fresh milk
6-8 small cardamom seeds

Put the grated carrots, sugar and milk into a non-stick
pan and cook over a low flame. The carrots will
slowly cook in their own juices. The milk will thicken
and when all the liquid has gone (1-2 hours) add
the butter or ghee and fry the halwa. Add sultanas.
Stir constantly to prevent sticking. Keep on frying
the halwa for 30 minutes. The carrots will turn a
reddish brown. Add the crushed cardamom seeds.
     Pour the halwa on a serving dish and decorate with
almonds. Can be served hot or cold.

Other Indian puddings

Gulab Jamum	Dark brown coloured sweets made of milk and flour served in sugar syrup
Qulfi	Indian ice-cream made with thickened milk and nuts
Rasmalai	Indian sweet made with separated milk solid and served in a sugar and milk sauce.
Rasgulla	Sweet white balls of milk served in sugar sauce.